The Hardest Working Letter

ERIN MORRISON

The Hardest Working

Letter

The Many Jobs of Silent E

For my reading intervention students,
who are also the most hardworking.

E. M.

ISBN: 979-8-866-65860-2

www.upandawayliteracy.com

Silent E is busy
with 9 big jobs to do.

It's the hardest working letter.
Let's learn why it's true!

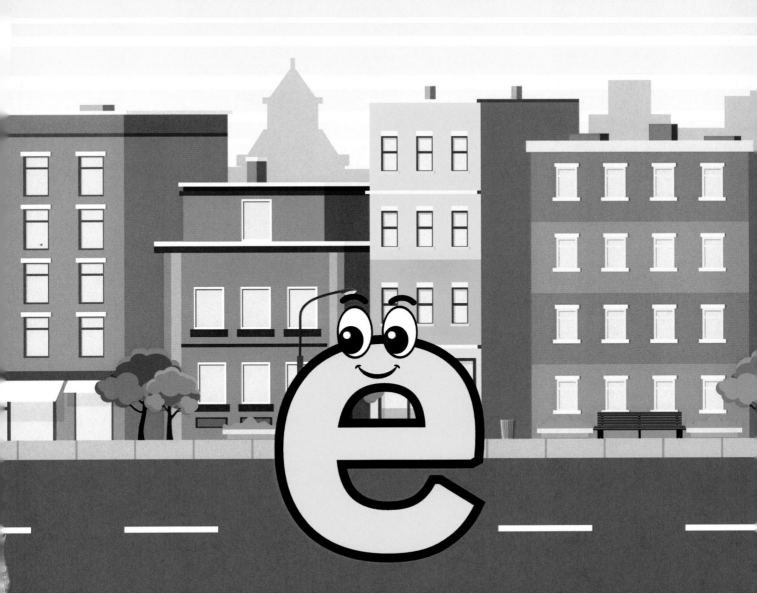

1

**Silent E can make vowels long,
like in hope and pine and game.**

hope pine

game

**When there is a vowel–consonant–e,
the vowel can say its name!**

In the English language, words don't end with i, u, j or v.

Whose job is to protect these letters?
Of course, the Silent E!

3 Every syllable must have a vowel
so for the consonant-le kind,

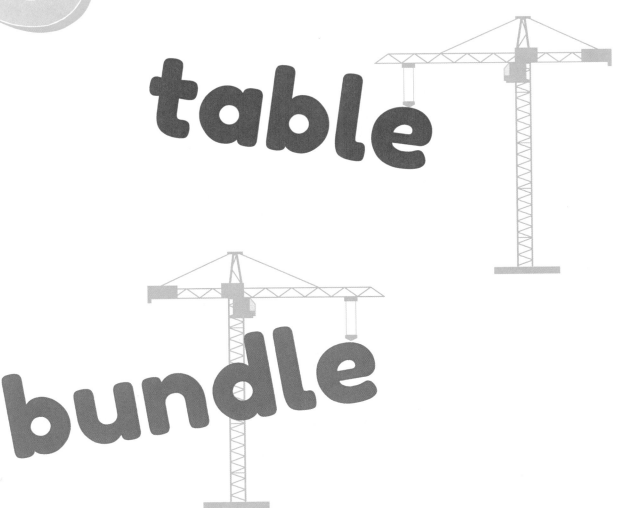

table

bundle

Silent E gets added on.
Now it follows the rule just fine!

Silent E can soften the sounds of c and g.

spice

dance

hinge

nice

**Like dance and spice, hinge and nice,
The sound is soft you see!**

5

**Silent E can also show
if a word is plural or not.**

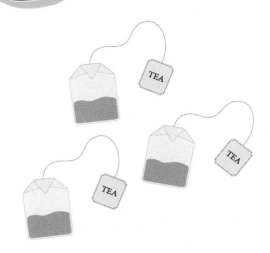

tease

**Dens or dense? Teas or tease?
The Silent E helps a lot!**

6

**Silent E can make TH
turn on its voiced sound.**

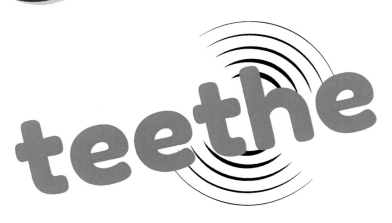

teethe

bathe

**From teeth to teethe and bath to bathe,
it's a noisy job all around!**

7 Silent E can clarify the meaning of words that sound the same.

Like by and bye, and aw and awe,
it's quite a claim to fame!

 **The Silent E can also make small words appear to be longer.**

If a word has more than two letters, it comes across as stronger!

 **Sometimes, Silent E shows the history of a word.**

It's doing an important job even though it seems absurd!

At the end of every day, Silent E has to rest.

Having 9 jobs can be tiring, even though it is the best!

Made in United States
Orlando, FL
09 July 2025

62792525R00017